Photographing America

As we all know, decisions are relatively easy to make but acting on them—seeing them through—sometimes proves more difficult, however firm the intent.

These words were prompted by thinking back to a few years ago, when a decision was made that committed us to photographing the United States of America. It was not a decision taken lightly; the country covers a huge area and it would probably take several lifetimes even to travel to every part of each of the states, without attempting to take any photographs—and certainly not the photographs we had in mind. Nevertheless, the decision was made, and a considerable amount of time was spent in discussing and planning the photography very carefully, so that a representative collection of pictures could be produced showing both the familiar and the not so familiar, as well as some of the little-known aspects of this fascinating and diverse country.

It quickly became apparent that, however the problem was viewed, it was one of enormous complexity. In order to show as much of the country as possible—and, of course, to its best advantage—weather conditions in the various states, north to south, east to west, had to be carefully considered, also taking into account the fact that seasonal variety would be necessary in order to create a balanced coverage.

Difficult though travel might be, because of the distances involved, and accessibility, because of the amount of equipment that would have to be carried, the actual photography was the least cause for concern. We knew that we had the best photographers, that they had the best equipment for the job, and we were confident that they would be able to produce the high quality, imaginative photography that we wanted. The real problem was one of logistics; how to make sure that the right photographer, with the right equipment and back-up, was in the right place at the right time.

We knew that no amount of planning, however careful, would cover every possible eventuality. A famous general once remarked to the effect that although every small detail of a battle could be planned, every counter-move by the enemy taken account of, there came a time when everything depended on the soldiers in the field and how they accomplished the task that had been set. So it was with this particular project.

Hotels were out of the question for many of the locations. We knew that it would be necessary for the photographer to be on site and ready to shoot, perhaps at dawn, at sunset, or maybe during the night, and eating and sleeping arrangements would have to be fitted in to suit the photographic requirements. Accordingly, campers were purchased, the idea being that a camper could be used by one particular photographer to cover a certain area at the appropriate time and then, when somewhere was reached that did allow a more static base, it could be handed over to another photographer for use in a different area. Enormous quantities of film had to be made available; few things are more demoralizing for a photographer than to be in the right place at the right time, only to find shooting impossible for lack of film.

Photographers like using, and produce their best work on, equipment they are familiar with; equipment they can operate without thinking and which they trust completely. This meant that there could only be a very limited degree of interchangeability of equipment between photographers. Therefore spare cameras, lenses, light meters and so on had to be carried so that, in the event of one item of equipment failing, shooting could still continue.

Arrangements were made for the airfreighting of exposed film back to base for processing, and for the photographers to be contacted to let them know that all was well—or not—with the results of their endeavours.

In the event, the project took three years to complete, and it is to the great credit of the photographers concerned—their tenacity, adaptability, imagination and professional expertise—that a truly outstanding collection of color transparencies was eventually assembled. It is from this collection that the photographs on the following pages have been chosen. The choice was difficult in that there was so much material to choose from, and many fine pictures had to be excluded, but we feel confident that the reader will agree that the final result was well worth the effort involved.

Creative Director
Colour Library International Ltd.

Washington D.C.

Washington D.C.

In the year of 1790, two of America's foremost statesmen, Thomas Jefferson and Alexander Hamilton, made plans to build a federal capital. A ten-acre site on the Potomac River was ceded to the government, thereby creating the District of Columbia. Today, Washington DC has an area of 69 square miles on the Maryland side of the Potomac River and a large tract of land on the Virginia side. The population now numbers over two million, a large number of whom work for the government.

The task of raising the money to buy the land and to construct the buildings was given to George Washington and he made an inspired choice of planner for the new capital when he appointed

The magnificent Capitol Building bottom right, *with its sweeping lawns and colorful flower beds, looks particularly impressive at sunset* opposite page, *resplendent against an orange sky.*

Among Washington's splendid monuments and buildings are the National Archives building below, *the statue of Thomas Jefferson* left, *and the Iwo Jima Memorial* below left.

Washington D.C.

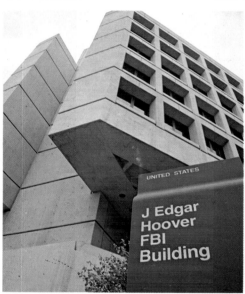

Washington D.C.

The National Air and Space Museum
far left top *is part of the Smithsonian Instititution and houses a fascinating collection of historic aircraft and spacecraft. The modern building* far left center *was named after J Edgar Hoover, long-term director of the FBI.*

Far left bottom *shows a reproduction of the famous Liberty Bell, while* above *are just two of the priceless exhibits in the Capitol Building. Many thousands of people visit the Washington Monument* top, *surrounded by fifty 'star-spangled banners' representing the States of America* left.

IN THIS TEMPLE
AS IN THE HEARTS OF THE PEOPLE
FOR WHOM HE SAVED THE UNION
THE MEMORY OF ABRAHAM LINCOLN
IS ENSHRINED FOREVER

Washington D.C.

a Frenchman, Major Pierre Charles L'Enfant. He was a veteran of the War of Independence and had served with Washington at Valley Forge, a site near Philadelphia where the army had endured terrible hardships during the winter of 1777/78. L'Enfant, who was an accomplished engineer and architect, envisaged a city of wide straight avenues with parks and squares and a Capitol building as the focal point. Many of his ideas were, however, scorned by Congress and he himself was ridiculed. It was only after his death that this talented man received the recognition that he truly deserved. His remains now lie in Arlington National Cemetery, which overlooks one of the most beautiful and impressive cities in the world.

One of Washington's best-known monuments is the Lincoln Memorial far left; *the Capitol is pictured* left.

One of the city's newest churches is the National Shrine of the Immaculate Conception top *with the Mormon Tabernacle* above.

New England

New England is a region in the northeast part of America comprising the states of Maine, Vermont, New Hampshire, Massachusetts, Rhode Island and Connecticut, which was named by Captain John Smith, an early English explorer and a representative of certain London merchants. The region was colonized by the Pilgrim Fathers who landed near present-day Provincetown, Massachusetts in 1620 in search of a better life. After signing the Mayflower Compact, they crossed the bay and founded the Plymouth Plantation. Soon more Puritans arrived, having escaped religious persecution in England, and within four years ten thousand had settled in Massachusetts.

The area in which the colonists settled was heavily forested, with numerous streams and rivers, the rugged coastline of which provided good, sheltered harbors. Some of the forest was cleared for farming and the timber sustained a flourishing shipbuilding industry. Saw and grist mills were constructed and fishing and fur-trading were also important.

Now a successful manufacturing region, New England is also renowned for its higher educational institutions, such as Harvard in Massachusetts, and Yale in Connecticut.

A rugged coastline punctuated by whitewashed lighthouses right is part of the characteristic charm of Maine, the largest of the New England states, and the Acadia National Park incorporates a series of beautiful inlets and coves.

The smallest state of New England, and indeed the nation, is Rhode Island. Its capital, Providence, has retained much of its original character, with buildings like the beautiful white Georgian marble State Capitol top right, and the delightful old church above. The city is an important deep water port and commercial center.

Vermilion, orange, russet and golden *hues flood New England's landscapes every fall. These warm tones light up the trees of maple, beech and poplar, a familiar sight in this densely forested region.*

Boating and fishing are two of Maine's most popular pastimes; left shows sailing boats and pleasure cruisers in Northeast Harbor. The region is one of rolling hills and tree-filled valleys studded with attractive towns and villages like Hartford, Connecticut bottom, Providence, Rhode Island far left top, and Woodstock, Vermont far left bottom.

New York City

In founding their own colony of New Amsterdam, on the site of the present city of New York, in the early 17th century, the Dutch also selected the best natural harbor on America's Atlantic coast. New York Bay itself had been discovered by an Italian, Giovanni da Verrazano, a hundred years before and explored by Henry Hudson, an English navigator who had been commissioned by the Dutch East India Company to find a shorter trade route to the Orient. When Hudson reached New York Bay he sailed up the river which now bears his name. From an ice-free harbor the Hudson River Valley provided an easy way through the Appalachian Mountains and, when joined by the Mohawk River, became vitally important as a link between the farms and factories of the middle west, the Great Lakes and New York City. This route contributed greatly to the development, from 1664, of New York, when New Amsterdam fell to the English without a fight, and was renamed.

In 1690 the population of New York was 4,000. Fifty years later

Amid the concrete network of a thousand skyscrapers, all jostling for space on Manhattan's crowded island, the Empire State Building, once the world's tallest, still towers supreme. One of the most impressive ways of viewing Manhattan is by helicopter. Not only can many of the skyscrapers be seen at close quarters, but the narrowness of the island becomes apparent and the tremendous amount of office and living space concentrated in such a small area is quite amazing.

30 Rockefeller Plaza

The dramatic Brooklyn Bridge, seen as night falls above, connects Manhattan to Brooklyn. The Rockefeller Center top left and right occupies a three-block site whose central skyscraper is the RCA Building. Paul Manship's huge, golden statue of Prometheus dominates the square, while the flags of many nations flutter gently behind it top right. The square houses an ice-rink in the winter, replaced by tables and chairs in the summer.

New York City

Amid the clamor and *confusion of the city lies Central Park below left and right. This lovely oasis was created by Calvert Vaux and Frederick Law Olmstead in the mid 19th century and they contoured the park to the natural topography of the area. With its ice-skating rink, open air theaters and restaurants, it is a haven to residents and visitors alike—840 acres of outstanding beauty in the middle of a concrete jungle.*

The fascinating street life of New York vibrates with people and traffic alike, but it is the architecture of Manhattan that makes the most lasting impression on the visitor; tall fingers of glass and steel, soaring upwards and creating canyons of the streets, parts of which remain in perpetual shadow. These skyscrapers influenced urban development throughout the world.

New York City

Fifth Avenue, New York's most fashionable shopping center bottom *is lined with exclusive shops.* Left *shows the unmistakable Statue of Liberty, given to America by the people of France to commemorate the alliance of the two countries during the American Revolution. This enormous statue—the figure is 152 feet high and the outstretched arm is another 42 feet long—has become the symbol of a new life and a new world to thousands of immigrants and exiles.*

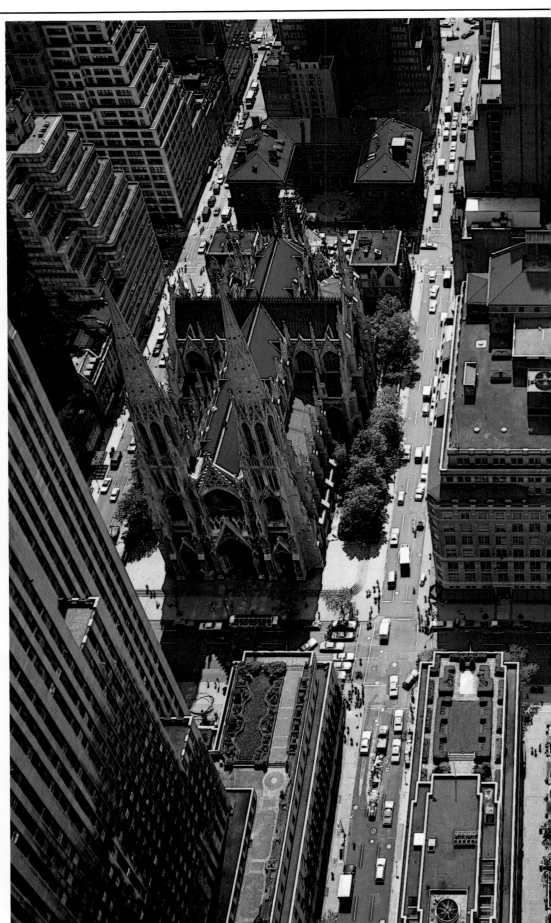

it was 11,000 and by the end of the 18th century approximately 28,000 people lived in this handsome and flourishing city. Its success was largely due to its ever-expanding trade with Europe and with the American interior, and its magnificent harbor was always crowded with ships loading and unloading. Today, the port handles an enormous amount of traffic.

Of the millions of immigrants who were attracted to the USA, many decided to stay and make their homes in New York. Their different languages and customs, which they have to a large extent retained, resulted in New York becoming one of the most cosmopolitan cities in the world. Within its boundaries are distinct districts, and overlooking them all is the unforgettable Statue of Liberty, which rests on its own island. This is a symbol not just of New York but of the whole of the United States of America.

St Patrick's Cathedral, with magnificent soaring spires, was designed after the noted Cologne Cathedral. It is seen left *from the dizzying heights of the RCA Building.* Far left *These pictures illustrate the diversity of life in New York.*

Below *Housing the offices of the Mayor is the majestic City Hall—one of the more traditional buildings in this ever-changing city, while* bottom *the famous banking center of Wall Street is seen from an unusual angle.*

New York State

Part of the living history presentations at North Hudson's fascinating Frontier Town are the costumed demonstrations above and the horse-drawn stagecoaches left.

New York State

The eastern part of the United States, now known as New York State, was originally settled as a colony of the Netherlands following Henry Hudson's famous exploration, in 1609, of the river which now bears his name. In 1624 the first permanent settlement in New York was established by the Dutch at Fort Orange, the site of the city of Albany today. The following year saw a similar colony called New Amsterdam—now New York—located on Manhattan Island, an island bought from the Indians for sixty Dutch guilders' worth of beads and trinkets.

By 1800 New York was the second largest state in the Union, but ten years later it led the others in terms of population, manufacturing, trade and transportation. In the 20th century, New York State ranks second to California in population, but continues to lead in many other fields.

Left *and* **below left** *The exciting steer riding rodeo and the 'Tribute to John Wayne Rodeo' attract many visitors to North Hudson. Picturesque Old Bethpage Restoration Village on* Long Island is another example of living history. Shown here are the dining room of Schenk House below, and a display of broom making bottom.

The border between Canada
and New York State is formed by
the Niagara River, which
provides the water for the most
popular of US attractions,
Niagara Falls, half of which,
known as Horseshoe Falls, are
actually in Canada.
Dramatically illuminated for
about three hours after dusk, the
American Falls can be seen
above *from Skylon Tower and*
left, top left *and* center left *from
the Observation Platform.*
Opposite page *The cascading
water creates a spectacular
rainbow in the bright sunlight.*

New York State

The state of New York is rich with beauty and history. Attractive Alexandria Bay below, with its lovely village harbor, is set in the Thousand Islands region, and contains many interesting sights, like Bouldt Castle bottom. The first church to become a basilica in the US, the magnificent Our Lady of Victory, Lackawanna, Buffalo, is richly decorated; its brilliantly painted dome is shown far left. Historic

Old Fort Niagara left and below center, situated at the mouth of the Niagara River, Youngstown, was originally built by the French in 1726, enlarged by the British, and finally completed by the Americans.

Philadelphia

The character of old Philadelphia is captured in the photograph left of Elfreth's Alley, lined with brick houses which date back to the 18th century when colonial blacksmiths, river pilots and tailors resided here. The cathedral basilica of Ss Peter and Paul right is the principal church of the Philadelphia diocese. Its construction was completed in 1864 and it was designated a basilica in 1976. The famous Liberty Bell was ordered from England in 1751 to commemorate the 50th Anniversary of the Charter of Privileges. It hung in Independence Hall for over 200 years.

William Penn arrived in Pennsylvania in October 1682. He had been given 28,000,000 acres of land there by a grateful King Charles II who also named the area 'Penn' after William's father, an Admiral. 'Sylvania' was added by William Penn and he crossed the Atlantic to found his 'perfect city' which he called Philadelphia. The spot he picked had a small harbor and beach and the land around it was high enough to be the ideal spot for a city.

He ordered that the streets of Philadelphia would be straight, and that they would all lead to the river. He specified that no houses should be built within 200 paces of the harbor, to leave room for a commercial center, and he asked that home builders center their structures on their building lots, leaving room for gardens and orchards so that it would be a 'green country town'.

Even 20th century industrialization has not been able to destroy his unique concept, and Philadelphia today is an attractive, thriving city which retains its original atmosphere.

Of all the immigrants who found their way to Philadelphia, the most famous is Benjamin Franklin, who left Boston in 1723. Throughout his successful career he always retained a fondness for Philadelphia, once called 'the most American of cities'.

Independence Hall above dates from 1732. It was in this graceful brick building that the Declaration of Independence and the Constitution were signed. The building stands on Independence Square.

Philadelphia

Top *The Franklin Memorial in the Franklin Institute pays tribute to the great philosopher, scientist and statesman who came to Philadelphia at the age of seventeen as a poor young man.*

A popular story recounts how a committee of Congressmen, headed by George Washington, went to the home of seamstress Betsy Ross, and engaged her to make the first 'Stars and Stripes'. Today, her tiny house in Arch Street above is famous as 'The Birthplace of Old Glory'.

Philadelphia

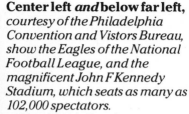

Center left *and* **below far left,** *courtesy of the Philadelphia Convention and Vistors Bureau, show the Eagles of the National Football League, and the magnificent John F Kennedy Stadium, which seats as many as 102,000 spectators.*

New Year's Day in Philadelphia is traditionally the occasion for the Mummer's Parade — an array of colorful pageantry which has its origins in pre-colonial times. This exhibit left is part of a permanent public display of Philadelphia Mummery at the Mummers Museum, who kindly provided the photograph.

Penn's Landing above, *extending from Market Street to Lombard Street, now boasts a wealth of modern developments. Dilapidated piers were demolished before the Bicentennial to be replaced by an extensive marina, walkways, parks, and even a helicopter pad. It provides an ideal site for boat shows and mooring for ships.*

Viewed from above, Philadelphia left emerges as an impressive conglomerate of glass and steel office towers and modern stadiums set among charming colonial houses. Surrounded by modern development, Independence Hall stands as a monument to a great American tradition. Inside Independence Hall, the Assembly Room has been restored to its appearance when used as a meeting place by the founding fathers.

Philadelphia

Outside the Museum of Art above *flutters the flag which was 'born' in Philadelphia. The museum's majestic columns are seen at the end of Benjamin Franklin Parkway* opposite page.

Right *Benjamin Franklin Bridge, one of Philadelphia's besk-known landmarks, spans the Delaware River from the city center to Camden. When it was built in 1926, it was the largest single span structure in the world, extending 8,291 feet from portal to portal.*

In Penn Square, at the intersection of Broad and Market Streets, City Hall far right, *houses the headquarters of Philadelphia's municipal government. Its 500 foot tower is dominated by an imposing statue of William Penn, who gazes down upon the city he founded in 1682.*

Cape Cod

Cape Cod offers mile upon mile of sparkling white beaches, a glistening bay, a rich and colorful marine life and picturesquely restored segments of a remarkable history. Dominated by magnificent land and seascapes, the different seasons exhibit a special magic all their own.

A prominent commercial fishing town, boats set out from Provincetown right every morning, to return later with their catches of cod, flounder and haddock. The harbor was the pilgrims' first port of call after leaving England in 1620, before moving on to Plymouth in search of more fertile farmland.

One of Provincetown's attractive weatherboarded houses displays the 'Star-Spangled Banner' top; flags flutter gaily in front of the memorial to James Otis above.

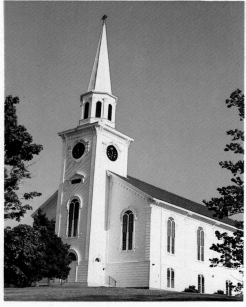

The historic towns of Cape Cod contain many beautiful buildings like the old windmill above, the stark white church top, and the colonial courthouse above center.

Cape Cod

Cape Cod

Discovered in 1602 by an English navigator, Cape Cod was given its name after the enormous schools of cod fish found there. Colonized in 1630, the Cape attracted many pilgrims and by 1646 four towns had been formed: Sandwich, Barnstable, Yarmouth and Eastham. Cape Cod is now one of the country's most loved holiday spots. An undeniably compelling place, its popularity has caused a great deal of change to take place over the past few years, but the new seems to complement the old. Offering three hundred miles of breathtaking coastline, the Cape is a sportsman's paradise and for those who prefer to relax, the climate is excellent and the countryside dotted with historic villages. To travel straight round the Cape would take perhaps two days, but few people would be able to resist spending more time exploring the sights—around every corner is something to delight the visitor.

The elegant building far left *is Brewster's Town Hall, built in 1880, which is set in leafy grounds. The Coast Guard Beach Center on Coast Guard Beach* below center *serves as an environmental and educational center.*
Fishing plays a large part in this area, and the delightful harbors are filled with brightly-painted boats and colorful characters top center *and* above. *The monument* left *honors the pilgrims who sailed into Plymouth aboard the Mayflower.*

Virginia

Virginia has one of the longest continuous histories of any American state, dating from 1607 when pioneer settlers arrived from England and landed at the site of present-day Jamestown. They named this part of the New World after Elizabeth I, the 'Virgin Queen', and it was an area which, under the original charter, included lands west of the Atlantic seaboard settlements, to the Mississippi river and beyond.

Virginia's pleasing climate and beautiful scenery attract countless visitors every year. The state parks and national forests provide spectacular views and many of the old tobacco plantations continue to thrive, carrying on the great traditions of those early and courageous settlers.

Historically, the state is exceptionally fascinating, with the triangle of Jamestown, Williamsburg and Yorktown containing a wealth of exquisitely restored 18th century buildings, whilst at Jamestown are full-size replicas of those first tiny vessels that landed in 1607 and were to have so much influence on the future of this American state.

Williamsburg, the capital of *the colony of Virginia between 1699 and 1799, was named after William III. Beautifully restored to preserve its 18th century appearance, its numerous houses, shops and buildings have been reconstructed on their original foundations. Throughout the seasons, visitors to Williamsburg can enjoy the presentations of the colorfully costumed Colonial Williamsburg militia company* right *and* below. *Displays by the company include drilling, special salutes to the accompaniment of fifes and drums, and tactical demonstrations of the muskets and cannons, which were used by the valiant troops who fought so desperately on Virginia soil to win their independence from the British Crown during the war-torn torn years of the Revolution. These exhibitions are among the most popular attractions in this area.*

This statue of James Monroe above *is sited in the boxwood garden of his estate at Ash Lawn. The impressive Governor's Palace* right *at Williamsburg, was both home and office for several royal governors.*

Virginia

The distinctive red Nicolson's Shop below *was originally used by Robert Nicolson as both a tailor's shop and store, and is typical of the charming clapboard houses in the area.*

Situated on 9th and Marshall Streets, and lovingly restored as a national landmark, is the only surviving 18th century brick dwelling in Richmond. Within the building are many original furnishings and family possessions which reveal the simple elegance of this lovely home. The stately dining room is pictured right.

Mount Vernon, George
Washington's beloved home, is pictured top; left is another example of the carefully-preserved buildings, this one in Fredericksburg, which contains a wealth of historic houses and museums as part of the nation's rich colonial heritage.

The beautiful home of Thomas Jefferson, Monticello above, is a classic example of American architecture—its dominating feature the white dome which commands the west front. The three-story building, comprising thirty-five rooms, is magnificently furnished and includes many of Jefferson's personal mementos. Today the gardens on the east and west lawns look much as they did during the time of Jefferson's retirement. Center Candle-making in the traditional way.

Atlanta

Atlanta is a city of great contrasts, and one which *has successfully blended the old with the new. The ultra-modern city center* right *contains Peachtree Plaza, whose lobby* above right *boasts a half-acre lake. The ghost town of Auraria* top *is a reminder of the extraordinary days of the Gold Rush.*

Atlanta

The thriving city of Atlanta, Georgia, started life as a small fort built by a team of 22 recruits, in 1813. Nearly 25 years later, a young railroad engineer, Stephen H Long, chose a location seven miles east of the Chattahoochee river as the terminal point for the Western and Atlantic line railroad.

The small frontier hamlet of Marthasville had quickly become a trading center for the surrounding countryside, and by the time the first train from Augusta rolled into town in 1845, it was thriving. The next few years saw a change of name from Marthasville to Atlanta and the blossoming from a small hamlet into an increasingly prosperous community.

Rebuilt after the Civil War, having seen crushing defeat and poverty, Atlanta has become one of the nation's busiest financial centers. Like its symbol, the phoenix (the mythological creature which was consumed by fire and rose renewed from the ashes) Atlanta has risen and been strengthened.

Sited in downtown Atlanta, Peachtree Center top left *is a magnificent complex which is virtually a city within a city. The colorful and exciting 4th July Parade dominates Atlanta's normally busy streets* above *and* top.

Atlanta

Opposite page top right *shows a stunning example of the beautiful mansions found here in Georgia; superb Plantation House* **bottom right** *and the covered wooden bridge* **center right** *stand in Stone Mountain Park, just outside Atlanta.*

The beautiful buildings **right,** *so typical of the architecture in Georgia, are part of the University of Atlanta.*

Many of the 'plantation plain style' buildings so prevalent in colonial America have been carefully restored by the Atlanta Historical Society, like the one shown **above.**

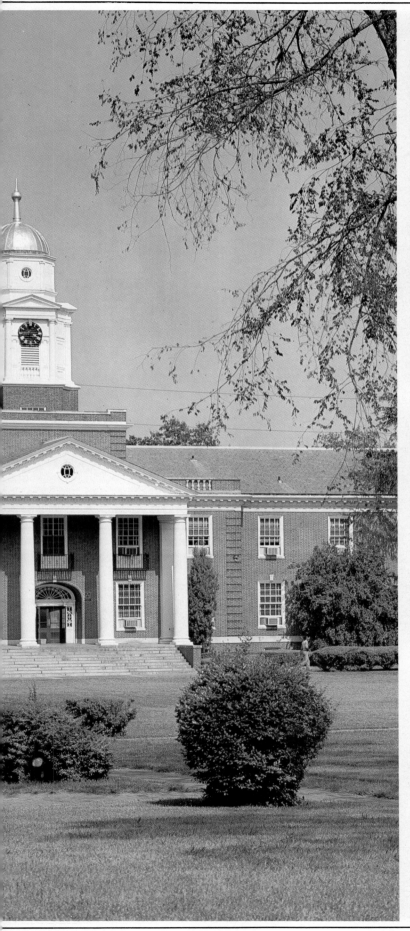

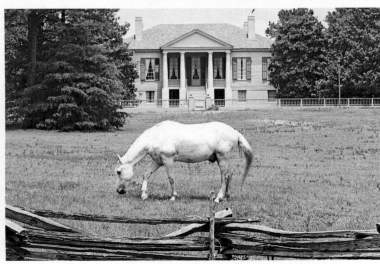

Atlanta

Atlanta

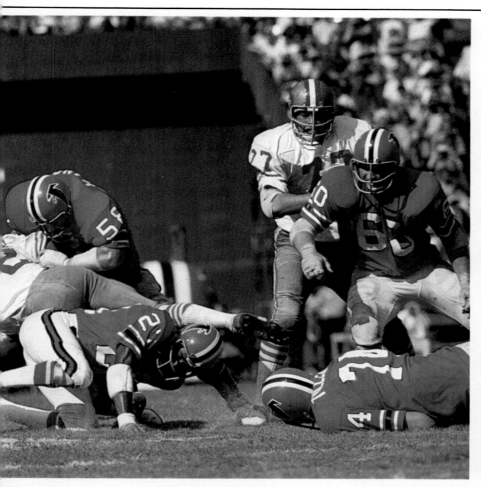

The magnificent Atlanta Stadium featured these pages *was completed in 1965, and it is here that Atlanta's professional baseball and football teams, the Braves and the Falcons, delight the crowds. Atlantans are enthusiastic spectators and participants in many sports, including soccer, tennis, golf and stock car racing.*

Florida

Florida

Twenty years after he is believed to have sailed with Columbus, the Spanish soldier and explorer Ponce de Leon first sighted the coast of Florida. The year was 1513 and in April he landed at St Augustine, claiming the country for Spain. He returned to his homeland a few months later to announce the discovery of what he had taken to be an island, and was given permission by King Ferdinand to colonize it.

When he returned he attempted to start a colony on the west coast, but it was to last for only six months and, during a skirmish in the struggle to survive, he received a severe arrow wound, of which he was to die in Cuba. For over 200 years, however, Spain remained in control of Florida, despite intermittent warfare against the English and the French, who were both eager to gain a foothold in this part of the continent, and against the Seminole Indians, the majority of whom were eventually sent to territory in the west.

One of the most fertile farming areas is in the south, along the southern shore of Lake Okeechobee. All around the lake, however, are the Everglades, an untamed marshland of cypress

Fifty years ago, Miami Beach was a wilderness of mangrove swamps, infested with snakes and mosquitoes. Today it is the largest resort in the world, attracting visitors from many countries eager to enjoy the luxury hotels, sub-tropical climate and fine beaches.

The clear turquoise water, white sandy beaches and dazzling hotels opposite page illustrate clearly the international appeal of this holiday playground.

Fort Lauderdale below is a popular winter resort for yachtsmen and fishermen alike. The city's deep water port at Port Everglades accommodates even transatlantic liners.

Typical of the old colonial architecture in the area, this attractive building top is situated in Key West, the southernmost city in the United States. Seaquarium above is one of Miami's most popular attractions, where killer whales perform a wide variety of tricks.

Florida

The photograph left *clearly* shows the changing tones and colors of the waters that lap the shore of ultra-modern Miami resort. The colors change with different light falling on them, from deep, intense greens to equally saturated blues.

Hollywood's replica of the 'Bounty' in St Petersburg Harbor *far right* is enchanting when seen by night.

Another spectacular marine life center is Sea World at Orlando in central Florida, where visitors can feed and touch some of the creatures below.

Yachts and deep sea fishing boats lie becalmed in their moorings at Miami Marina *above* as twinkling lights shine against an evening sky. As in other American cities, skyscrapers are very much a part of the Miami skyline.

In the heart of Florida are the breathtaking Cypress Gardens, where spectacular blooms can be seen all year round. The towering cypress trees and the evening sun glinting through the leaves make a beautiful picture as they line the shimmering water's edge of Lake Eloise *right.*

Florida

The incredible Disney World these pages *has undoubted appeal for the whole family. Filled with exciting exhibits, and the best known and loved of Walt Disney's characters, Disney World delights its visitors, particularly the children. A circular tour of the entire magical kingdom can be taken on an old-fashioned steam train* above, *while the riverboat* top *plies the extensive waterways. The perennial Disney favorites, Donald Duck, Mickey Mouse and Pinnochio, make a great trio* above center. *A prominent late night feature is the dazzling firework display which fills the sky with vibrant colors as the firecrackers explode high over Cinderella's Castle* right.

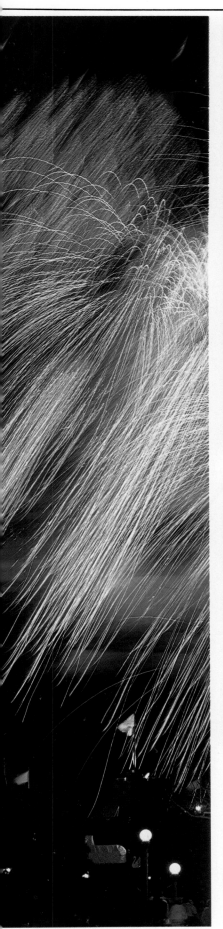

At night Disney World takes on *an even more magical quality and Cinderella's Castle, enchanting against the black velvet sky, is a breathtaking sight for child and adult alike.*

Looking down Main Street towards the castle top, *the lights twinkle in this most wonderful of wonderlands.*

and gum trees set among wide stretches of saw-grass, harboring snakes, rare birds, alligators and a diminishing number of American crocodiles.

As a holiday state, Florida has a great deal to offer. The focal point is Miami and its island city, Miami Beach—the largest and most dazzling resort of all. Giant hotel and apartment blocks glint in the bright, reliable sunshine and are reflected in the warm, blue waters of Biscayne Bay and the Atlantic Ocean. Incredibly, the buildings that we see today were built on a wilderness of mangrove swamps, infested with mosquitoes and snakes. This southernmost state of the USA is certainly a land of plenty for both visitor and resident.

The Old South

It is almost four hundrd years since the first English pioneers arrived in Jamestown, Virginia, eager to start a new life. They introduced a plantation society that spread rapidly throughout the southern states of the USA—a society that for two centuries made great fortunes but also introduced slavery into the thriving tobacco and cotton fields. The Civil War changed everything: thousands of lives were lost, vast areas were devastated and four million slaves suddenly found themselves free—but with nowhere to go. Poverty was rife, but slowly the south was rebuilt and today it is challenging its northern neighbors in the fields of commerce, industry and politics. Much of the Old South, however, still remains, retaining the atmosphere and warmth of southern hospitality, and the charm of the several nations that influenced it.

For eight years, Mobile, Alabama, first christened Fort Condé, served as the capital of the French colonial empire, and today the elegance of this early French influence is reflected in its wrought ironwork, its beautiful gardens and its fine old mansions. Gaineswood, Demopolis is one of the finest Greek Revival structures in the south. Its interior below is still furnished with period pieces.

At Middleton Place, America's oldest landscaped garden, the main house is surrounded by a profusion of exotic trees and butterfly lakes straddled by slender bridges. On the brink of a mirror world, the Rice Mill right stands perfectly reflected. Many of the picturesque buildings in the area have been reconstructed on their original foundations.

Drayton Hall right is just one of the elegant buildings for which Charleston, South Carolina is renowned. Charleston itself was built on a peninsula between two rivers and overlooking one of America's finest harbors. The city has a unique heritage of stately houses and fine public buildings, carefully preserved today in the style and condition of two centuries ago.

Longwood, one of the most extravagant of the millionaire mansions of Natchez, was the dream of Dr Haller Nutt, although it has never been completed. During the Civil War, Confederates burned his cotton fields. He fed and clothed Union troops, who in return set his cotton gin, three plantations and sawmill alight. Dr Nutt died of a broken heart. His widow tried to survive by selling milk to the northern soldiers, who proceeded to steal her cows. Part of the interior is seen above.

The Old South

Top *A serene river reflects the* *delightful city of Charleston.*

In the National Military Park, Vicksburg, Mississippi, the proud figure of a soldier right *commemorates the Confederate dead, and* above *cannon still line the ridges that once resounded with the clatter of war. The American Civil War, fought between 1861 and 1865, started successfully for the* southern states, known as the Confederates, but after their defeat at Gettysburg in 1863, which was the turning point of the War, the northern states (the Union) quickly gained ground, and the South was devastated. Remaining spiritually and economically downtrodden for the following eighty years, the South is now enjoying a period of reconstruction.

The soft, fibrous masses of the cotton balls on the cotton plants below *recall the days when many of the South's beautiful buildings first came into being* right *and* below right. *Cotton superseded tobacco as the South's most important crop in the 19th century, after the invention of the cotton gin, and the new states of Alabama, Mississippi, Louisiana and Texas benefited*

especially. The cotton millionaires built exquisite mansions and lived a sumptuous lifestyle. The gracious living of those times can be seen in many of the carefully-preserved houses, like the National Russell House left, *constructed in 1809.*

Texas

Until 1685, when a French expedition led by Robert Cavelier founded Fort St Louis on the Texas coast, the region had been controlled by the Spanish. Cavelier's colony did not survive for long, though, and by the 1730s the Spanish administered a network of missions and forts throughout central, east and southwest Texas, the center being San Antonio. By 1845, Texas was admitted to the United States, after lengthy battles with Mexico, who themselves had declared independence from Spain. One of the most famous battles in American history was fought during Texas' struggle for independence from Mexico—the seige at Alamo.

The state joined the Confederacy in 1861, but rejoined the Union in 1870. By 1900, the cattle industry was flourishing, railroads had been built, manufacturing grew and the population of the state had reached three million. Just one year later, the Spindletop oil field was discovered, and Texas' petroleum industry was born.

Texas is now an agricultural and technological leader; its cities are among the most dynamic and fast-growing in the country; and its landscape is one of the most beautiful and diverse, with mountains, forests, lakes, rivers, and subtropical beaches, and of course the famous prairies.

Dallas top right and bottom right and opposite page top right, the state's second largest city, is also the southwest's largest banking center, a leader in wholesale business, and among the leaders in 'million dollar' companies. A transport and communications hub, the skyline of Dallas is filled with soaring skyscrapers that rise from a web of ultramodern highways. This well-planned metropolis is a noted cultural center with a fine range of theaters and auditoriums, and extensive shopping and sporting facilities; its sleek, glossy office buildings contrasting with gracious suburbs and green parks.

Texas

Austin left, *the state's* sophisticated capital, is a modern, progressive city, with unquestioned historic stature. Surrounded by dense green foliage, the majestic pink granite State Capitol building stands at the heart of the city. Once the riverside village of Waterloo, built where the River Colorado crosses the Balcones Escarpment, Austin became a center of research and development. The noted educational establishment of the University of Texas, founded

in 1881, played a major role in Austin's growth and development. Beyond the Littlefield Fountain above rises the imposing twenty-one story tower of the university's administrative building, a famous Texas landmark. The city was the first American settlement in Texas, and was named after its founder, Stephen F Austin.

Texas

Among Houston's many fine sporting facilities is Summit Stadium right, *where enthusiasts can watch their home team in an exciting game of basketball* below *and* below center. *Houston is also the home of the NASA Lyndon B Johnson Space Center, situated near Clear Lake on a 1,620 acre site, with about 100 different buildings. One of the newest and largest research development facilities, the center is a focal point of the Nation's manned space flight program. Among the exhibits on view to the public are the Travehicular Mobility Unit* far right, *the Moon Buggy* center top, *and the flight articles* center below. *Attracting thousands of visitors every year, the Space Center provides a fascinating insight into the area of space travel.*

LUNAR MODULE TEST ARTICLE
LTA-8

Texas

Right *Flags flutter proudly in*
the breeze outside Summit
Stadium. The Huntsville prison
Rodeo below *includes such
spectacular events as bull-riding
and saddle and bareback bronco
riding. The Texans are famous
throughout the world for their
cattle industry, and although the
longhorn* opposite page below
right *has been usurped by other
breeds, Texas beef and dairy
cattle still play an important part
in the state's economy. Shown*
center right *is a cattle auction at
Amarillo; the town has retained
its 'Western' atmosphere—the
brightly colored stage coach*
below right *advertises a steak
ranch.*

Texas

The Alabama-Coushatta Indian
Reservation provides colorful evidence of the state's historical heritage; the reservation is located in the heart of Sam-Houston National Forest. Beyond the concrete congestion of the cities lie the beautiful rugged Hill Country and the Pernales State Park on the banks of the Pernales River left.

The railway station **center left** *and St Joseph's Church* **far left** *in San Angelo recall the days when the town grew up as a center of early ranching efforts. The founder of Dallas, Neely Bryan, lived in this log cabin on Elm Street* left.

Texas

Texas

The USS Texas, only survivor of the Dreadnought class, has been moored at San Jacinto since 1948 *opposite page. The symbol of a state's wealth and prosperity for the future, the stark lines of an oil rig are silhouetted against a bright orange sunset* below. *Reflected in the dark, still waters, fireworks create an unforgettable display* bottom left, *while the chorus line* bottom right *kick ever higher.*

Arizona

Begun in the autumn of 1971, the construction of the village of Tlaquepaque below *and* bottom *was the realization of the dream of Abe Miller, a Nevada businessman who was inspired to build an arts and crafts village in Sedona, Arizona. In a setting of spectacular natural beauty he created charming shops, galleries and restaurants mainly in the style of Spanish colonial architecture, decorated with red roof tiles, flower pots, bells, statuary and wrought iron-work imported from Mexico. Phoenix, Arizona's sophisticated capital, is the home of beautiful St Mary's Church* right.

In the several thousand square miles that constitute Monument Valley, isolated monoliths of red sandstone tower as much as 1,000 feet above the sandy wasteland below *and* below right, *where the stunning sunset was used to brilliant effect by the photographer providing a tremendously dramatic backdrop. One of the principal remaining ruins to be found in the Canyon de Chelly National Monument is the White House* bottom right *which was actually occupied from 1060 to 1275.*

The Arizona of the 1970s with its modern cities and nationwide transportation arteries presents a very different image from that traditionally associated with the state's eventful frontier days. Yet not far from the metropolitan centers of Phoenix and Tucson the cowtowns, trading posts and Indian villages still stand among awesome natural scenery which has changed little since the first Spanish explorers ventured here in quest of the fabled golden cities. Eerie ghost towns still huddle among primeval petrified forests, snow-capped mountains and dramatic gorges, and carving its way through Arizona's northern plateau, the Colorado River still winds through the 'awesome abyss' of the spectacular Grand Canyon... one of the most majestic, colorful and awesome natural features of the world.

Like Arizona, New Mexico possesses an abundance of dramatic scenery, shaped by volcanic formations and strangely eroded rocks. Against the timeless beauty of its expansive plains and rugged mountains the contemporary state with its space-age search for new energy sources has also preserved much of its traditional heritage in a daily blend of Indian, Spanish and Anglo cultures which reflects both yesterday's achievements and today's technology.

Grand Canyon

Grand Canyon

Mules, **opposite page top** *provided the ideal means of transport along these narrow, winding cliff paths. In the course of some six million years the Colorado river seen* opposite page center *from Lipan Point, has cut 5,000 feet down into the rock, and differences in the relative resistance to erosion in the succeeding layers of stone have given the walls of the South Rim the rough, step-like form seen* opposite page bottom *from Mather Point.*

One of the world's most *awe-inspiring features is surely the Grand Canyon* left *and* above, *where two thousand million years of earth building lies exposed in the stratified rock that lines this most spectacular of the nineteen gorges along the Colorado River. The panoramic views from observation areas like Hopi Point and Mohave Point give the onlooker a truly unforgettable experience.*

Arizona

Arizona

The Pueblo de Taos with its *carefully maintained church* opposite page top *and terraced communal dwellings* opposite page bottom *tells of a culture hundreds of years old.* Opposite page center *shows the Kit Carson House and Museum. Oak Creek Canyon* below *is one of many canyons which cut into the Colorado Plateau. Indians still make their traditional homes in Monument Valley* left. *A scene in Tlaquepaque village, Arizona* bottom.

Ohio

Ohio is one of America's Midwest states, that vast area of rolling countryside and endless small towns which provides the nation and many other parts of the world with meat and grain.

Known as the 'Buckeye' state, Ohio is also highly industrialized with cities like Cincinnati, Cleveland and Toledo producing an enormous variety of goods. Over the years the state has provided the country with eight Presidents and three Vice-Presidents, two Hollywood cowboys, Roy Rogers and Hopalong Cassidy, and entertainers such as Bob Hope and Phyllis Diller. Yet overall Ohio's population reflects an ethnic mix, established in the early 19th century when steamboats plied the Ohio River and canal and railroad building was in its infancy.

Today Ohio faces the problems that affect all heavily populated areas around the world: pollution of river, lake and atmosphere, avoidable waste of natural resources, crime and poverty in inner cities and traffic congestion. However, an intensive program to correct these problems is well under way, in an attempt to preserve an acceptable quality of life for Ohioans. The photographs on these and the following pages illustrate why Ohio is a state well worth taking good care of.

With a host of attractions for the whole family including over fifty thrilling rides, Cedar Point in Sandusky right *and* bottom, *which boasts the largest marina on Lake Erie, is considered to be mid-America's finest entertainment center.* Below *is a superb night-time photograph of Cincinnati's magnificent downtown area. The exotic 'Arcade'* opposite page *connects two of Cleveland's major thoroughfares.*

Ohio

Pictured right *is a peaceful roadside* farm at Somerset. Western Ohio is famous for its great corn belt and picturesque farms like the one shown center bottom *off Highway 50. Abundance and plenty are the* first words that spring to mind on encountering these bountiful fields. Situated at Old Wright Field, Dayton's US Airforce Museum displays an outstanding *collection of exhibits* below.

Pictured above *is Cincinatti's famous Taft Museum.* Opposite page *is a view of the sleek governmental buildings which line the east bank of the Scioto River in an impressive landscaped setting. Columbus actually lies at the confluence of the Scioto and Olentangy rivers and the city was named in honor of the famous early New World explorer.*

The Twin Cities

The Twin Cities

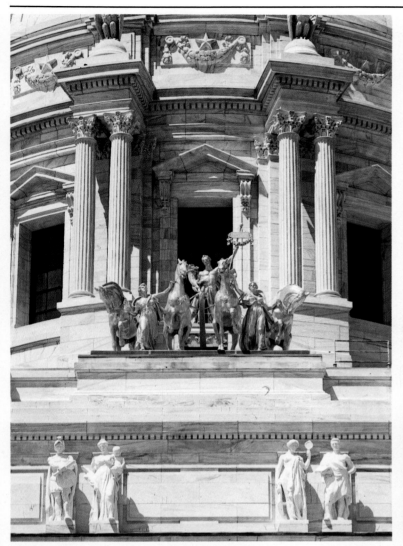

Minneapolis and St Paul, the Twin Cities, lie in the state of Minnesota, in the heart of the North American continent. The quality of life in this part of the USA is admirable, for not only have the major problems of other urban areas been avoided or resolved, such as bad housing, poverty, soaring crime figures and traffic congestion, but cultural amenities, theater, music, art and education are all of the highest order and the facilities for outdoor recreation are superb.

In character the Twin Cities are vastly different. Minneapolis, the largest city in the state, is both cosmopolitan and inventive, with a wealth of beautiful parks, glittering lakes and a skyline of striking new buildings. One of these, the 51 story, prize-winning IDS Building, has an all-weather Crystal Court containing shops and cafés enhanced by shrubs and flowers, which is linked by glass enclosed bridges to other city blocks; an effective measure to combat Minnesota's severe winters. In contrast, St Paul, the state capital, is conservative, and life there is greatly influenced by Yankee and Irish Catholic traditions. It is also an attractive city with its share of modern skyscrapers, but its real charm lies in the tree-lined avenues and stately old mansions, one of which was the home of the writer F Scott Fitzgerald.

The glittering Minneapolis skyline is seen opposite page *from the junction of the 1-94 and 280 freeways. The silhouette is dominated by the glass-sheathed, 775 foot high IDS. Tower. The majestic State Capitol in St Paul* left *has been the center of Minnesota State Government since 1905. Within the building can be seen the exquisite Rotunda Dome* below left. Far left *is shown the sculpture group, 'The Progress of State' at the base of the Capitol's dome.*

The Minnesota Twins, seen in an action-packed game versus Milwaukee at the Metropolitan Stadium right, *first boosted the baseball scene in 1961 when, as the former Washington Senators, they moved into the area.*

The Twin Cities

A view of the interior of Minnesota's Capitol is shown right, looking through the center of the building. The superb statue of the 'Father of the Waters', which stands in the foyer of City Hall opposite page top, was carved in Florence in 1905 by Larken Goldsmith Mead, from a single piece of Carrara marble. The majestic cathedral of St Paul is constructed of St Cloud granite—the lovely interior is illustrated below. The elegantly appointed rooms center and opposite page center and bottom depict Minnesota's rich Swedish heritage—they are among thirty-three rooms contained within the American Swedish Institute, the former mansion home of Swan J Turnblad.

Wisconsin

Wisconsin

Wisconsin, one of the most appealing vacation states of the USA, displays a magnificent and varied range of majestic scenery—from undulating landscapes in the south to densely forested regions along its northern border. Crystal clear lakes and streams provide outstanding opportunities for fishing and canoeing, and with the unique Door County peninsula, lovely Lake Michigan shores and a wealth of national parks and forests, offering scenic splendor and historic sites, the state plays host to countless vacationers all through the year.

Discovered by Jean Nicolet, its early history was closely associated with the lucrative fur-trapping trade; and with developments in lead mining, lumbering and diversified farming and dairying, the state flourished.

From the frontier came tales of the legendary Paul Bunyan, the mythical, gigantic lumberjack who was said to have fashioned Wisconsin's topography and, aided by his redoubtable ox, Blue Babe, and Johnny Inkslinger, sheared the state of its virgin timber.

Today this progressive state maintains an excellent balance between its important manufacturing interests, agricultural industries and tourism, while its well-planned cities, such as Madison, the state capital, and Milwaukee, the commercial hub, are also noted for their fine, cultural institutions.

Sentinel straight, brightly colored pink, purple and white lupins line Highway 13, north of of Wisconsin opposite page. Wild flowers are characteristic of this lovely state and north of Rhinelander, along Highway 17, they bloom in profusion—a riot of orange and gold left. A tranquil scene outside Lynxville is shown top left. Above A fisherman proudly displays his catch of wall eye pike, while below, a familiar sight in this predominantly agricultural state.

Wisconsin

One of Milwaukee's most *distinctive landmarks is the Mitchell Park Horticultural Conservatory* above *which features three conoidal glass domes, each 85 feet high and 140 feet wide. They have separate, artificially-controlled climates and display exotic, tropical blooms, unusual desert specimens and changing seasonal flowers. The exterior of City Hall, Milwaukee is shown* top, *displaying fine Flemish-Renaissance architecture.*

Wisconsin

Farms, and acres of arable farmland dot the fertile countryside of this wide and varied state where agriculture is basic to the economy. North of Chippewa Falls, which has developed as a trading center for dairying and agricultural products, are picturesque farms left.

Below is pictured the Old North Point Water Tower in Milwaukee seen behind a brilliantly-illuminated fountain.

A spectacular aerial view of the Wisconsin river can be seen bottom as it winds through the thickly-forested area of the lovely Dells region.

Wisconsin

Wisconsin

Madeline Island, which seems to float in the beautiful blue waters of Lake Superior, can be reached by car ferry. The historic town of La Pointe is noted for the Madeline Island Historical Museum top, the interior of which contains artifacts relating to the history of the area, documented on the marker above.

Left The Villa Louis at Prairie du Chien nestles in an idyllic setting provided by its beautifully landscaped grounds.

With a wealth of state parks and beautiful recreation areas, the state offers a magnificent variety of unrivalled scenery.

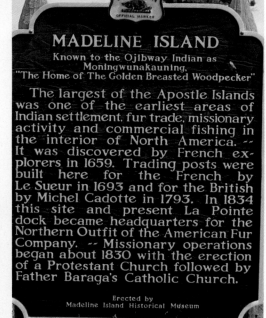

The leafy, tranquil greenery of the Hartman Creek State Park near Waupaca is shown opposite page top and bottom.

The photograph below left captures the contentment and peace of a scene where little boys fish in the silver waters of Lake Metonga at Crandon.

Chicago

Chicago

Home of the skyscraper, the Encyclopaedia Brittanica, Wrigley's chewing gum, Pullman cars and McDonald's hamburgers, Chicago also boasts the tallest building and the busiest airport in the world. Another famous name associated with America's second city is that of Al Capone, but his violent era is long past and Chicago is no more the crime-ridden city it once was, when people feared to walk its streets. Instead it is a thriving business center, important for banking and finance, manufacturing and retailing. The name Chicago derives from an old Algonquin word —Checagou—which can mean, variously, 'wild garlic', 'skunk' or 'skunk run'; none of which can be applied, in the 20th century, to the Chicago that has grown from an isolated army post to a vast, sprawling urban area with lofty skyscrapers, industrial plants and a network of vital roads and railways. However, moderating this conurbation are beautiful parks, outstanding museums and gracious, stately buildings. There is, in addition, a magnificent skyline that looks out across the broad, blue waters of Lake Michigan, a lake that provides tranquillity, recreation and a doorway to this teeming city.

The superb aerial photograph opposite page *is of North Lake Shore Drive, and dramatically captures both land and sea...Students stroll through the leafy grounds which form an integral part of the Widebold Hall University Complex* left.
The Chicago Police boat regularly patrols Lake Michigan, the third largest of the great lakes and the only one completely contained within the confines of the USA. Bright yellow taxis are a familiar sight in Chicago far left. *One of Chicago's most exquisite landmarks is the Bahai House of Worship* center *whose dome is a masterpiece in stone tracery.*

Chicago

Day or night, Chicago is a tremendously exciting *place to be—the skyline dominated by huge buildings* left, *while night-time* above *is even more spectacular. Here is shown the awe-inspiring Sears Tower which occupies a full city block and stands over 1,468 feet high.*

Right, center right *and* bottom right *are scenes illustrating Chicago's Maxwell Street Market—as colorful as the characters who buy and sell there!*

The Northern Rockies

Majestic, snow-capped mountains, crystal clear lakes and streams, huge forests of conifers and dazzling waterfalls are part of the magnificent scenery of the Northern Rockies, where vast national parks and forests teem with an abundance of wildlife and a profusion of flowers.

This too, is the land of the 'Wild West'—pioneer country where thousands traveled the famous Old West Trails in search of a 'promised land', or combed the mountains in quest of gold. Once thriving communities, which sprang up in the gold-rush era, and which for years lay derelict and abandoned, have been carefully restored and reconstructed and, together with informative museums, provide the visitor with a compelling glimpse into one of America's most stirring and colorful periods.

Large areas have been designated national parks and forests, and it was here that the nation's first, superb Yellowstone National Park, was established in 1872. Although primarily in Wyoming, its 3,472 square miles extend into the states of Montana and Eastern Idaho, offering spectacular scenery and unsurpassed facilities for outdoor recreation.

South Pass City above *was once a prominent gold rush 'boom town' of the mid-nineteenth century. It achieved major national significance through Esther Hobart Morris, whose pioneering determination resulted in the State of Wyoming becoming the first government in the world to grant equal rights to women.*

At the Buffalo Bill Historical Center at Cody, there are four museums, one being the Plains Indian Museum right, *where there are a series of exhibits representing the Plains tribes.*

The Northern Rockies

Montana's Glacier Country is an area of *unsurpassed beauty. Above is shown a tranquil scene at North Fork on the Blackfoot River;* below *Swan Lake and* bottom *the Ross Creek Giant Cedar Grove.*

Left *is an astonishingly atmospheric view of Jackson Lake and the Grand Tetons seen from Signal Mountain.*

Yellowstone

Yellowstone Park offers the visitor special trips through part of its magnificent landscape *far right. The* trips take the form of thrilling stagecoach rides which leave from Roosevelt Lodge. This Park is famous for its astonishing geysers. In the Upper Geyser basin are located spectacular hot springs which intermittently spurt hot water into the air. Old Faithful *far right* is the most publicised. The concept of a hot, steaming river never fails to fascinate and the illustration *right is a scene to be* found in the Midway Geyser Basin, where steaming water cascades into the aptly-named Firehole River. Skeletons of trees stand sentinel in Black Sand Basin *below.*

Throughout Montana, 'The Land of the
*Shining Mountains', majestic ranges dominate
the landscape, as seen beyond St Mary's
Mission at Stevensville above.*

*Below is shown the somehow mysterious
ghost town of Elkhorn, located in the Elkhorn
Mountains.*

The Northern Rockies

Beautiful Lake McDonald above **reflects** *a pale blue sky.*

The force with which Firehole Falls tumble earthwards below *results in a constant steamy haze which serves to enhance their beauty. These azure-blue waters* bottom *belong to Hoback River in Wapiti Valley, Wyoming.*

The Northern Rockies

On the floor of a dense forest in Avalanche Gorge blooms the delicate queencup lily *left, a tiny reminder that beauty can be found wherever you look!*

Far left pictures the sheer faces and aloof summits of Garden Wall, *their grandeur subtly swathed in gray-blue mist.*

Piercing the brilliant blue skies are the jagged peaks of Mount Oberlin and Mount Cannon below. *Mount Oberlin is featured again* bottom, *this time in a stunning view taken from Logan Pass.*

Los Angeles

The modern Los Angeles is a city filled with architectural and engineering showpieces linked by broad boulevards throbbing with an interminable flow of traffic and charged with an excitement that has earned it the title of the 'Prototype of Supercity'. This is the city too of glamorous Hollywood, the fabulous center of the film industry and of glittering Beverly Hills, home of the movie stars whose luxurious mansions provide a glimpse of opulence among the palm trees that line the hillside avenues. Nowhere, it has been suggested, is the pursuit of happiness more unabashedly materialistic. Banks, saving and loan associations and insurance companies stand on what was once a land of vineyards, orange groves and dairy farms, and nightclubs, fashion houses, hotels and stores offer a sparkling array of dream-wares in settings designed to capture everyone's secret fantasies.

Yet behind the fantastic façade lies a more seriously motivated city with outstanding cultural and educational facilities, a sophisticated convention center and carefully planned freeways that provide ready access to the natural beauty of golden beaches washed by the waters of the Pacific.

The photograph right is an almost abstract portrait of the flags which lend color to the imposing heights of Century City. The modern face of Los Angeles is reflected in its glossy buildings and expansive highways— traffic races past the Wiltshire Building above.
In Chinatown above right Los Angeles forsakes its sleek, modern image for a strongly oriental feel presented here in a neon-lit pagoda-style building.
In the forecourt of the Chinese Theatre, Hollywood, the footprints, handprints and signatures of yesterday's movie stars are a famous attraction far right.

The city of Los Angeles *boasts a seemingly endless stream of night spots and clubs, like the Playboy club* right *and* above. *In the heart of Los Angeles lies the Pueblo* this page center left *and* top left, *whose Mexican village atmosphere is* at its most pervasive in Olvera Street, with its colorful market stalls and street musicians. Presenting a different aspect of the city is the graceful City Hall above right *in afternoon sunshine.*

Los Angeles

Los Angeles is a summertime *city and its mild, sunny climate encourages all manner of outdoor activities—sporting or otherwise.*

The wonderful, magical world of Disneyland at Anaheim is captured on these pages. All the favorite Disney characters are here—Mickey Mouse, Donald Duck, Tigger—and they delight children and adults alike. Two exciting methods of transport here in Disneyland are the monorail and the enchanting Mark Twain Riverboat opposite page top right, *which cruises down the river passing Tom Sawyer Island and Fort Wilderness.*

California

San Diego is California's southernmost city and has a wealth of attractions for both visitors and residents. In the lovely Balboa Park are superb examples of Spanish baroque architecture below while above is picturesque Sherman Gilbert House dating from 1887.

California

The fabulous J Paul Getty
Museum below *was built in the style of a 1st century Roman villa and houses a marvelous collection of antiquities and paintings. California is justifiably famed for its wonderful sunsets, and one only has to look at the photograph* left *showing the sun setting behind Pigeon Point Lighthouse to see why. La Jolla, caressed by the deep blue Pacific* opposite page bottom *has a stunning coastline which has been compared with that of the French Riviera. Palest gold sandy beaches, white surf and an idyllic climate make La Jolla a sought-after holiday retreat.* Far left *is a view of Old Point Loma Lighthouse.*

California has the largest, richest and fastest growing population of all the American states. For over two hundred years people have been attracted by one of the finest climates, some of the most beautiful scenery and acres of the most productive farming land in the world, not to mention large deposits of gold and oil. In fact it was from the rich gold mines that California earned her nickname 'The Golden State'.

California is also renowned for fruit farming. Enormous areas of the Central Valley provide ideal conditions for the growing of apples, plums, oranges and peaches, as well as for vineyards from which America's finest wines are made. The hot, sunny summers ripen the fruit, and water from the great Sacramento and San Joaquin Rivers is used for the necessary irrigation systems.

These rivers have their source in the majestic, snow-capped Sierra Nevada to the east, where some of California's most outstanding scenery is to be found.

The huge numbers of people who have chosen to make their homes here have, of course, affected the land itself. Concrete highways and huge skyscrapers, smog and pollution all leave their mark. Nevertheless, the natural world still predominates, and man's awareness of the fragile beauty which surrounds him is resulting in an effective protection program for this beautiful state.

California

One fifth of the state of California is desert these pages. *This arid land is divided into two national monuments and one state park. The state park is called Anza-Borrego, a lonely, hot region of shifting sands and cacti, which, when in flower, provide welcome splashes of color in an otherwise barren, but nevertheless beautiful, landscape. Far right* are the *brilliant pink blooms of the prickly pear.*
Death Valley National Monument holds fourteen square miles of undulating sand dunes and eerily lonely views can be seen from Zabriskie Point, such as these dune-like mountains center right.

Spring brings a shock of color to Death Valley *below* while *bottom is the imposing, fort-like structure of Scotty's Castle set amid inhospitable mountains.* Opposite page bottom left *is pictured the chiseled rock formation of Red Rock Canyon in Kern County* while *opposite page bottom right,* looking like a sheet of crazy-paving is the Bristol Dry Lake near Amboy in San Bernadino County.

California

The spectacularly lovely coastline at Big Sur in Monterey *is illustrated* right *and* far right, *as the Pacific Ocean, in gentle mood, laps the coves. The old missions of Southern California are part of its rich heritage and nowadays many are centrally placed within the cities that grew around them. Below is the whitewashed mission at Santa Barbara with its picturesque pink relief.* Bottom *in tranquil setting is the Mission of San Luis Obispo. Opposite page top left is Mission San Buenaventura which has elegant tiled fountains gracing its gardens.*

California

***Hearst Castle** left and below left perches on top of San Simeon's 'Enchanted Hill'. The place is dominated by a building called La Casa Grande, and the estate boasts terraced gardens with marble statues, pools and guest houses. The swimming pool featured here is graced by a real Greek temple, imported and reassembled here.*

Below can be seen another view of the lovely Mission San Buenaventura. The delightful courtyard of Mission Juan Capistrano is shown bottom. The church was founded in 1776, American Independence Year.

San Francisco

Perched on the hills above the often mist-enshrouded Golden Gate Bridge lies the colorful and cosmopolitan city of San Francisco. It appears as a mass of white buildings, crowned by several skyscrapers, that cling to the hillsides and sweep down to the shores of the Pacific Ocean.

The city dates from 1776 and it was a trading post in 1846, when it was captured by United States forces during a war with Mexico. In 1906 an earthquake almost completely destroyed it but it was subsequently rebuilt into one of the loveliest cities in the world. San Francisco has twenty-one hills plied by the famous cable-cars. Nob Hill, where in earlier days rich people lived in ostentatious mansions, is probably the best known. Today the mansions have gone, and in their place there are towering hotels and apartment blocks. At the bottom of the hill is Union Square, where elegant and sophisticated shops are situated and close by is the fascinating Chinatown area, which has the largest Chinese settlement outside the Orient and which contains some of the finest restaurants in America.

As a symbol of San Francisco, the Golden Gate Bridge is one of the most spectacular sights in the world. Although it is no longer the world's longest suspension bridge, its graceful structure never fails to impress and perhaps the bridge can be said to be a reflection of the strength and beauty of this extraordinary city, a city where many people leave their hearts.

Oakland Bay Bridge **opposite** page, *with its suspension and cantilever sections both double-decked to accommodate a huge volume of traffic, connects Alameda's capital and seaport of Oakland with San Francisco. Many of the skyscrapers afford magnificent views of the city, but surely the most exciting of all these buildings is the Transamerica Pyramid* above *and* left. *Top left is an aerial view of Berkeley University.*

San Francisco

Standing under the south tower of Golden Gate Bridge, historic Fort Point above *was built in the mid-nineteenth century to guard the Golden Gate. There were 127 cannons installed but none were ever needed. The view* top *shows clearly how the Oakland Bay Bridge connects to Yerba Buena Island and the city of Oakland beyond.*

Broadway right, *with its blazing lights, clubs, bars and restaurants attracts many visitors although some would say it is but a poor imitation of the original Barbary Coast which emerged in the days of the gold rush in California.*

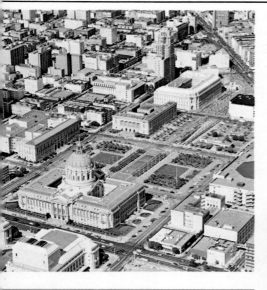

Fisherman's Wharf above **is** one of San Francisco's top attractions, with its hundreds of little boats, seen here with Coit Tower in the background.

An unforgettable sight – sunset floods Golden Gate Bridge right.

During the last twenty years San Francisco has become an important financial center and consequently a city of soaring skyscrapers which serve to enhance the charm of the old – the gracious, domed City Hall seen above left.

San Francisco

San Francisco is probably the most cosmopolitan city in the world and for resident and visitor alike it is entirely different from any other American city. On the hills are row upon row of distinctive Victorian houses all painted in bright colors. There are impressive skyscrapers, tempting restaurants and exclusive shops, ethnic neighborhoods and their associated foods and festivals. San Francisco is all this and much more.

Synonymous with San Francisco are cable cars far right, *this one seen silhouetted on the skyline at the top of the almost-vertical Fresnol Street.* Left *is shown the sublime interior of Stanford University's Memorial Church which dates from 1883.*

The majestic Golden Gate Bridge is shown right. *Below is an entrancing night-time shot of Oakland Bridge seen against a glittering back-drop of city lights.*

The Colorado Rockies

Four hundred years before Columbus made his epic voyage to America, a race of people inhabited a maze of stone-built cliff dwellings in south-west Colorado. Many of those homes still remain, but their occupants moved away long ago. As time passed, tribes of Red Indians, whose names—Cheyenne, Comanche and Kiowa—will be familiar to many afficionados of the Wild West, settled in the east, on the rolling plains of America's 38th state. To the west loomed the Colorado Rockies with their towering peaks, lush valleys and mighty rivers that had carved spectacular canyons as they made their way to the sea.

The discovery of gold and silver changed the face of Colorado's mountains in the heady days of the Gold Rush, when fortunes were made and lost with alarming rapidity. Small settlements grew into cities and the railroad penetrated vast areas of this previously isolated state.

Today, many people visit Colorado to escape the rigors of 20th century living, to enjoy the facilities of first class ski resorts like Aspen and Vail, and to appreciate the truly magnificent scenery of the many national parks, which are among the finest in the world.

The massive pinnacles of Mount Antero are seen under an ominous sky top right *while* top left *can be seen the peaks of Sheep and White Horse Mountains reflected in the still waters of Island Lake near Marble.*

Colorado has many ghost towns above *dating back to prospecting days. Colorado's most famous lake is the lovely Maroon lake* opposite page. *The shimmering blue water* right *is part of the beautiful Blue Mesa Reservoir in the Curecanti National Recreation Area. A sea of palest yellows and greens floods the hills around Ashcroft near Aspen* far right *and* above right.

The Colorado Rockies

The horizon line is made up of the lovely Sangre de Cristo Mountains *bottom. These mountains provide the perfect backdrop to the spectacular Royal Gorge in the Pikes Peak region, which is spanned by the world's highest suspension bridge. The famous Georgetown Loop Railroad* below *was originally opened in 1884. It connects the towns of Silver Plume and Georgetown.*

High on the slopes of Cheyenne Mountain is the Will Rogers Shrine of the Sun *right pictured against a sapphire-blue sky. It is an imposing fortress-like tower constructed of local gray-pink granite and dedicated to the memory of the famous humorist. Center right* The Black Canyon of the Gunnison *derives its name from the fact that little sunlight finds its way into the shadowy gorge.*

The Colorado Rockies

The old ghost town of Ashcroft is featured below, showing abandoned equipment and cabins which are now preserved by the Aspen Historical Society.

The symbol of the USA is the bald-headed eagle left seen here at the Cheyenne Mountain Zoo.

Beautiful lakes stud Rocky Mountain National Park. Nymph Lake bottom is seen dammed by sun-bleached tree trunks.

The Colorado Rockies

The Colorado Rockies

By using the high, spectacular and sometimes terrifying jeep trails below visitors can explore the ramshackle remains of the once-thriving communities of Animas Forks near Silverton, Tomboy on the Imogen Pass and Alta near Telluride. The lovely photograph left was taken from the thickly-forested banks of Maroon Creek, as the aspen leaves were taking on the golden hues of fall.

From Monarch Pass can be seen this magnificent vista of Tomichi Creek right. The fabulous ski-center of Steamboat above is sited in Steamboat Springs, Colorado. A perfect world can be seen reflected in Beaver Ponds in Hidden Valley left.

Washington State

Horses stand on the shore of scenic Lake Chelan *above. In the popular tourist attraction of Winthrop, rows of wooden-fronted houses, wood sidewalks and old fashioned street lights echo bygone 'boom mining' days* top *and* above center. *Lupins provide a riot of color in the meadows of Paradise during the summer* far right. Right *is a scene of rolling fields of unripened grain seen from Steptoe Butte.*

Washington State

Lofty mountains and sagebrush flats, wild rivers and alpine meadows, sweeping forests and a myriad of clear, blue lakes predominate in the Evergreen State of Washington.

Larger than the whole of New England, this northwest state remains largely unchanged since the golden era of the fur trade, when trappers became rich from the sale of beaver, badger, fox and racoon skins, and the Hudson's Bay Company was supreme.

The forests they roamed remain, many of them virgin timber due to careful lumbering; benefiting both the economy and the large number of tourists who come to enjoy their scenic splendor.

Dominating the state are the snow-capped peaks of the Cascade Range, which extend from British Columbia south into Oregon, and the mighty Columbia River, harnessed for irrigation and power by the Grand Coulee and other great dams, yet teeming with salmon and trout.

Washington's chief city is Seattle and, although it is an important port, and the gateway to the Orient and Alaska, its setting is one of great natural beauty, with a background of mountains and overlooking the Puget Sound.

Washington State

Two faces of Seattle can be seen above *and* top. *On the one hand there is the colorful market at Pike Place where stalls groan under their burden of produce and all sorts of unusual, and exotic, foods can be purchased; on the other there are Seattle's soaring skyscrapers, and the stunningly modern Space Needle which rises 600 feet above the Seattle Center. From the Needle's* observation deck can be seen *impressive panoramic views. Three views of Olympic National Park are shown* right, above right *and* top right. *This lovely park embraces majestic lakes, dense rain forests, mountains and stretches of stunning coastline.* Opposite page *The peak of Mount Rainier rises to height of 14,410 feet, seen here from near Paradise.*

Washington State

The reflection of Seattle's landmark, the Space Needle, can be seen top *in the shimmering facade of the Safeco Building;* below *it is seen from the Pacific Science Center.* Above *is an unusual view of the Monorail and the Washington Plaza Hotel.*

Washington State

The magnificent Cascade Range *separates the damp coastal region from the arid interior. Top features Liberty Bell Mountain and Early Winter Spires at Washington Pass on the North Cascades Highway. Above center is a view of Mount Rainier seen beyond a meadow full of summer flowers while above Narada Falls are among the many sparkling waterfalls that cascade over creviced rocks in Mount Rainier National Park.*

Left *This stunning photograph pictures remote Glacier Peak visible in the distance beyond the snow-filled canyons of the Cascades.*

Hawaii

Hawaii

On the map of the world, the Hawaiian archipelago appears as tiny dots in the middle of the Pacific Ocean. Together, however, these tropical islands form the 50th State of the U.S.A., a state that prospers from tourism and the export of sugar and pineapples.

The thriving state capital and port of Honolulu, with its famous Waikiki beach, is the hub of life in Hawaii and offers all the amenities of a modern American city. Honolulu is situated on the island of Oahu, and just a short flight away is the island of Kauai, where Captain Cook first landed, and Maui, where the largest dormant volcano in the world is to be found.

Thus it is not hard to explain the attraction of Hawaii, a state with something for everyone. Its scenery ranges from spectacularly rugged and mountainous regions, where there are active volcanoes, to white sand beaches washed by sparkling blue Pacific waters. There is also lush tropical vegetation with shower trees, poincianas, plumerias and jacarandas to dazzle the eye, and exotic fruits such as papayas, guavas, passion fruit and litchis whose very names are sufficient to stimulate the taste buds and which ripen to perfection in the hot, reliable sunshine.

The fabulous photograph opposite page *offers us a glimpse of heaven and illustrates more successfully than a thousand words ever could the beauty and magic of these enchanted islands. This* picture was taken at sunset in Ala Moana Park.

The Nahi Mau gardens left *are renowned for their beauty, and cover almost thirty acres of the Waiakea Peninsula.*

The Hanalei River left *meanders between green and fertile meadows. An important crop grown here is the taro plant whose roots provide a nourishing food.*

A giant bronze Amitabha Buddha above *is the focal point of the Jodo Mission's Buddhist Cultural Park.*

Hawaii

The most beautiful waterfall *on Kauai tumbles down a lush green cliff face right. This spectacular natural wonder is called Opeakaa Falls.*

Maui Island is the second largest in the Hawaiian group and is named after a demigod who, as legend tells us, fished the Hawaiian Islands out of the sea. Above is pictured a natural arch to be found in Maui's Waianapanapa State Park.

Kauai Island is the greenest of this group of islands and is consequently known as the 'Garden Island'. It is renowned for its fabulous beaches which include Barking Sands top.

Many exotic and brilliantly colored flowers can be found in Hawaii: left is a delicate Chilean jasminum and bottom is the exquisite Vanda orchid. More than 20,000 varieties of orchid grow on these islands. Surfing below is one of the most popular sporting activities in Hawaii.

A colorful state echoed by its equally colorful residents center left.

First English edition published by Colour Library Books Ltd.
© 1984 Illustrations and text: Colour Library International Ltd.
99 Park Avenue, New York, N.Y. 10016, U.S.A.
This edition is published by Crescent Books
Distributed by Crown Publishers, Inc.
h g f e d c b a
Colour separations by FERCROM, Barcelona, Spain.
Display and text filmsetting by ACESETTERS LTD., Richmond, Surrey, England.
Printed by Cayfosa and bound by Eurobinder - Barcelona (Spain)
ISBN 0.517.441047
CRESCENT 1984

Dep. Leg. B. 3.118/82